Cordolium

M.L. Fenix

BookLeaf
Publishing

Presentation by *BookLeaf Publishing*

Web: www.bookleafpub.com

E-mail: info@bookleafpub.com

ISBN: 9789395756389

First edition 2022

DEDICATION

I'd like to dedicate this book to all the friends and family I have in my life who've supported me through everything. For reasons of privacy, I won't name anyone here. I'd also like to dedicate it to my cat, who is always willing to spend time with me even when I'd rather be a loner.

The Millennial American Dream

I have my house with land all around,
flowers and trees planted into the ground.
I have enough money for what I need and want,
whenever I desire I can go to a restaurant.

I have money saved away,
if I need for a rainy day.
I don't worry about how I'll retire,
thoughts of the doctor don't make me perspire.

I afford a child if I want to,
I don't work till the day is through.
I have time for friends and a social life,
my job doesn't give me strife.

Trust Issues

False tales and lies cover my eyes,
when others use them as a disguise.

I always tried to believe everyone was good,
wanting to believe people were just
misunderstood.

I never regret putting faith in a new person,
feeding right into false promises and coercion.

I just want people to say what they mean.
the world would be less chaotic and more
serene.

How to Become an Addict

I can't go to the doctor,
I don't have money to pay the bill.
I can't afford the doctor,
but it's cheap for an illegal prescription pill.

I balked at the thought at first,
before the pain became too much.
I don't have time to be nursed,
my bank account was bust.

At first, they just get me through the day,
but the night becomes painful too.
The pills control my life.
Thoughts of the doctor? Through.

The Sun and the Moon

There once was a tale of the Sun and the Moon
who loved each other,
their children were the Stars and the oldest were
a pair of twins, a sister and a brother.

The Sun ruled with fairness for she was so
bright,
but she missed her lover who was only seen at
night.
She needed an heir and as the twins grew older,
it became clear whose burden it was to shoulder.

The Sun made the announcement to the Stars
and Moon,
that their leader would be the daughter as she
came first.
The boy filled with so much rage he felt he
would burst,
while the girl filled with regret that she would be
a queen soon.

"I am the North Star, the Guiding Star in the
sky,"
the brother thought, "how can my sister be more
powerful than I."

"Not me," the sister thought, "I want the chance
to experience love.
I don't want to be stuck, I don't want to just
watch others from above."

The girl was still young so she absconded and no
one saw to intercede,
the boy saw the heir was gone and his heart was
filled with greed.
The mother saw her mistake and withered away,
the son saw an opportunity and was here to stay.

Trying to hold on

Time slips through my fingers,
Months feel like weeks,
Years pass in a blink,
A morbid game of hide and seek.

I want to hit pause,
Savor the moments,
Acknowledge the flaws,
Find the missing component.

I don't want to change anything,
Just stop and stare,
Pretend that people who have gone,
Are still there.

2020

Make sure your mask is in place,
Firmly covering half your face.
Don't forget the vaccine,
Or hide inside and never be seen.

Classes and work on Zoom,
Quarantine inside your room.
Six foot distance away from me,
Check for new info from the CDC.

People stock up in the grocery store,
Something you can't do if you're poor.
Shelves are empty and others yell,
Earth's become a living hell.

A Break from my Anxiety

I opened my book and became consumed,
interruption occured and I resumed.
Leave me here inside another place,
reality's not something I want to face.

This book is my only escape,
from what Fate saw fit to shape.
I just don't want to think or worry or fret,
this is the only break my head can get.

Even when I sit there alone I list,
there's no way to resist.
My only way to relax,
is with a book and snacks.

The Goblins of the Glade

They came to take me like bandits in the night
Their green, ugly, skin gave me quite a fright.
They had a ritual, you see,
That needed a boy just like me.
They placed me in front of a fire,
Building it higher and higher.
My heart began to fill with dread,
I feared that I would soon be dead.
The smallest came up and with a growl and a
rumple,
He started to say words in a low spoken
mumble,
"My people need your assistance.
We know of your peoples resistance,
To work with the Goblins of the Glade.
They fear our people and are afraid.
We mean you no harm though,
That's the first thing you should know.
We just need a peice of your hair of snow,
It's imperative for our crops to grow."
I gave them the hair and went on my way,
And never told anyone about the Goblins that
day.

Schizophrenia

Mom, why can't you see the delusions are all in
your head?
Why can't you spend time with your kids and
grand kid instead,
You'd rather have nightmares of rape,
Make everyone out to be someone you hate.

You held on so tightly I had to escape,
Everyday you'd yell and berate,
Making sure I knew,
I'd never be as perfect as you.

Now that you've been alone for so long,
I wonder if you'll ever change the tune of your
song,
If you'll spend the rest of your days mentally
unwell,
Living inside your own personal hell.

Feminism

First, your right to an abortion is taken away.
Second, once you're married you can't leave
anymore.
Third, the girls can't testify in court.
Fourth, they change where you can go or work.

Eventually, you won't be able to choose what
you wear or say.
You'll have few choices about what to do with
your life.
All because men are strong and women weak.
Women should follow men like sheep.

If only women were outraged, angry, or mad,
It wouldn't be as easy to take their rights.
But women were afraid of men before this,
History on repeat like it's always been.

Change

Some are scared of starting again,
I see it only as a new adventure.
Somewhere unknown that I've only just begun to
understand.
I'll learn new things about the world and myself,
Try to focus on the positives and negate the
negitives as they come.
No matter how old I get,
I hope when it comes time to change again,
That I'm not scared and greet the new adventure
like an old friend.

Wanting to be Lonely

With joy, family and friends are a blessing.
However, with pain they are a retraumatization.
Making me relive the event again and again as
they question, what happened?
I'd rather cry in peace and pick myself back up.
Not see the pity in their eyes as they think of
what I've been through.
I never saw myself as a victim and worked
through my pain.
But the mirror reflection of me in their heads
captures me in that moment,
When I'd rather let it pass.

The Beanstalk

A man comes by and takes the cow,
I wonder what will I do now?
Another man comes and says here's a magic
bean,
I wonder, whatever does he mean?

When I get home I lie to mother about how,
I was robbed of the dumb, big, cow.
I tell her I traded it for a magic bean,
She tells me I'm as stupid as I seem.

She threw the bean away,
I went outside to work the rest of the day.
When I woke after sleeping through the night,
I saw a miraculous, wonderful sight.

A beanstalk had grown all the way to the sky,
I thought, how lucky am I?
Mother always gives me all the work,
While she just stands there with a smirk.
She always beats me with a broom,
So I climb the beanstalk cause she'll be awake
soon.

The Last Dragon

I walk into the cave, filled with apprehension.
I have to steal the dragons hoard to be a hero.
In reality, I only feel like a coward full of fear.
She looms in front of me, blue as midnight,
sparkling like a night full of stars.
How could something this beautiful, be the
savage beast I seek?
They sent me to kill her, the last of her kind.
Her eyes are open as I approach, watching, yet
she doesn't move.
She doesn't attack or try to fight me, her eyes
full of sorrow and sadness.
It must be horrible to be the last of your kind, I
think to myself.
Instead of an act of hate, I begin to see it as a act
of mercy.
My sword raises above my body.
She doesn't make a sound as I end her suffering.

Building the Future

Rolling into them, their hand on my back.
Calm fills me, despite the pain in my arm.
Peace shouldn't come, in another person.
It's a cruel joke.
The world screaming, "you can't do everything
Alone!"
But look how far being alone has got me.
Look at all I've done;
Building a future that I actually want to see.
If I sink into them forever, I'll forget about
building.
If I give in to peace, I'll have to leave
behind the anger that got me this far.
I'll become but a fragment,
of all I was achieving.
In return for a castle, I'll only get a home,
A family and love.
Sometimes though,
That doesn't seem enough.
My castle is safe and the walls are high,
I made sure of it.
No one but me can go inside.
Because what I'm scared of isn't strangers,
but what's inside the people I love.

The Moon

I stare at your beautiful and luminous shape,
Wish I could travel to you just to escape.
You sit there in the sky night after night,
Shining down your dull moonlight.

The stars shine beside you full of wonder,
Except on nights full of thunder.
There's been debate whether you're a girl or boy,
All I know is you bring me joy.

The Ghost

I watch over everyone I left behind.
I'm stuck in a place they can't find.
I've passed away long ago,
One winter day in dirty snow.

I'm sure they forgot about me,
No one visits my grave anymore.
Now I wonder around and just be,
Since life has shut the door.

I don't see other dead people around,
If they're here, they can't be found.
I'm lonely in this place beyond,
With no one to talk to or respond.

Miscarriage

The raindrops fall, splattering on the glass
Some days feel like they'll never pass,
Like the day I was told you were gone,
I became so angry, tired, and withdrawn.

I'd never see your little face,
Never feel your wonderful embrace,
Never get to see how you'd grow up,
My heart became an empty cup.

Where once there was hope,
I'm now going down a slippery slope,
All I feel is numb,
As into my grief I succumb.